SCREENWRITING GOLDMINE

Phil Gladwin has worked as a script reader, script editor and screenwriter since 1995.

He has been hired by (and sometimes been fired by) the BBC, ITV, and many different independent production companies to write or edit TV shows such as *The Sarah Jane Adventures*, *Grange Hill*, *Holby*, *Trial & Retribution*, *The Bill*, *Casualty*, *Murder City*, *Bugs*, *Red Cap*, *Crossroads*, and *Berkeley Square*, plus a good few others that never made it to broadcast.

Born in Grimsby, back in the olden days of the early 1960s, he has also worked as a cycle courier in central London, a researcher in Artificial Intelligence at Cambridge University, a waiter in London, Brighton and the East Village, and a technical writer for an IBM systems software house.

He loved being a cycle courier, but possibly his least favourite job of all was being the man who sat outside a massive freezer keeping tally of the movements of tons and tons and tons of frozen fish.

He now lives in Brighton.

SCREENWRITING GOLDMINE

How to write a screenplay
people are desperate to shoot!

Phil Gladwin

SCREENWRITING GOLDMINE

63 Lansdowne Road, Hove, E. Sussex, BN3 1FL

First published in 2007 by

www.screenwritinggoldmine.com

For Fran and Nancy

CONTENTS

CONTENTS

Introduction

I once got really angry with my agent. Real, bile seeping, coffee cup flinging, head pounding on wall angry. He had dared to suggest some rewrites for a screenplay that had sold twice, but hadn't made it to production either time. Feet on desk, hands behind his head, beatific smile across his face, he had dared to utter one highly loaded phrase. He had dared to say: 'writing's hardly rocket science, is it?'

Bombshell. Things between us crash landed. I shed him, like a hand grenade sheds its shell. How dare he?

But, now I've several years perspective on the row, I am big enough, I have the heart enough, to be able to admit: He was right. Reworking a script isn't rocket science. If you know what you are doing.

That's a very important If.

"If you know what you are doing..."

No-One Knows Anything

If you've spent any time trying to write, and you've got any kind of internet connection at all, you will have realised there are a million other writers out there hacking away at screenplays, all apparently convinced they know what they are up to, and shouting like wild animals at anyone who dares disagree. They sound so authoritative, so compelling, so right - and yet so few of their screenplays ever get past the first hurdle of the initial slush pile reader, let

5

alone to the desk of anyone with any commissioning power.

Meanwhile the people who do sell scripts seem to go on selling, and selling. Common sense would tell you they are doing something different. Common sense would tell you that what they are submitting to the production companies is quantitatively different to what you are submitting.

How hard can it be to work out what the differences are?

As you probably know, it's very, very hard.

In fact it's so hard it took me years to crack.

I've been writing for over twenty years and selling my screenplays for more than ten. I've been on course after course, I've done the gurus, I've read yards of How To Write Screenplay books – but most of all I've been working as a professional screenwriter in the British television industry and selling screenplay after screenplay.

In this book I'm going to give you the road map I've evolved and synthesised from a thousand different sources and endless experiments - the actual road map I use when I write.

I've developed 14 clear stages, or stepping stones, I follow religiously when I'm writing a new screenplay.

Follow the steps conscientiously and you WILL see results.

What is a Screenplay?

Ingmar Bergman once said words to the effect that his scripts were skeletons waiting for the flesh and muscle of images.

He is the master, and he sees it perfectly. When you write a screenplay you are building a skeleton. The bones are made from the changes in your characters' emotions over time. If these emotions are not true, and strong, your script will feel weak and unformed.

You are building a structure composed of emotional through lines. These through lines need to curve and cross in certain places so that they form a structure that we all recognise as a story.

If that sounds confusing, don't worry, it's probably just that you have never thought of a script in this way before. It's quite simple, really. Just stick with this book, and it will become clear.

Follow The Method

This is a complete method, which will take you from blank page to the end of a decent first draft.

You need to do each of the steps in order - and it's crucial to allow each of them the proper time. No rushing, or skimping.

If, after reading the book, you are disturbed by the amount of work I'm going to ask of you, well, I'm sorry to be the first to break it to you, but that's what it takes.

But if you start to do the work, you'll find it's the best possible thing there is for a writer – each stepping stone completed is another step closer to having a good screenplay finished.

So go ahead. Follow the Fourteen Steps. Read, absorb, do, succeed…

Step 1: Get Some Seeds

So there's just you and this blank page that you can't seem to get a foothold on. Where on earth do you start?

You should do one or all of the following, as long as necessary:

❖ Think about people you know, and have:

- Loved

- Been dumped by

- Been intrigued by

- Hurt

- Been Hurt by

- Felt sorry for

❖ Lie in the bath. Lie in bed. Lie on the sofa. Let your mind drift. Get into a state of semi-lucid dreaming. Wait for an image, or a character, or an event to pop up and make itself unforgettable.

❖ Think about things you have always wanted to see in a movie. Things that make you go Wow!

❖ Think about things that fascinate you. What are you obsessing about this week?

❖ Browse through old magazines and look at the photos. You need magazines with a strong human interest angle. I prefer newspaper supplements. The National Geographic can be useful sometimes too.

9

❖ Go to your bookshelves. Find a book you liked. Liked a lot. Think to yourself – is there any bit of it I loved so much I want to give it new life?

❖ Think about films you've have seen. The same question. Any parts of that story that you loved, and want to get into your story? An opening? A character? A story twist? A story structure? [1]

Somewhere in all that thinking there will be a starting point. By which I mean an image that interests you, or moves you, in a way that means you can't get it out of your head. A picture, an event, a situation between people.

What is Drama?

Make it easy on yourself though and make sure this picture always includes people.

That's because the only definition of drama that works is 'Character in Conflict', and by far the best place to find complex, interesting characters is people.

---

[1] Oh, and if you're bothered by the thought that these last two suggestions seem like cheating, or stealing, please don't be. For one thing, this is a practical, warts and all insider's account of how writing is really done. For another, Shakespeare 'stole' many of his plots, and professional producers and writers 'borrow' plot moments all the time. (That may explain why so much of modern screen drama feels so terribly over familiar, but that's another discussion!) Anyway, by the time you've finished your screenplay you should be about a million miles from your original source. Whatever you used in this way will have been long since absorbed and made new by your new work.

10

Pictures Not Words

But you should avoid moments that are all about conversations. You're looking for a real, concrete, in the world picture:

A man standing over a body with a bloody broken bottle. A kiss between mother and child. A kiss between two men. A young child painting a picket fence in scorching sunlight. An emaciated man being forced to walk barefoot over broken glass. A young woman blowing the dust off a long buried wooden chest.

Let your imagination run wild. But make sure there is a picture there. And make sure you personally find the picture absolutely charged with emotion. When you think about this image it should make you cry, or raging mad, or sick, or terrified to your core.

And don't worry about what other people might think of your ideas, just be honest to yourself. If you surprise yourself in admitting something you didn't know about yourself, great. Follow that thought!

Write It Up

Get this picture down in the word processor of your choice. I use Word for Windows, but it really isn't important which package you choose.[2]

Write without self censure, just free associate round that image till you run out of steam. How long you spend on this is up for grabs. You have to do fifteen minutes, or you haven't begun to put in the work. After a couple of hours I am rung dry and have

---

[2] www.Openoffice.org supplies a powerful and free word processor.

nothing left to say even about the most intriguing image.

Now, as much as you can, forget about that image.

Get back in the bath, get back in your bed, go for another walk, whatever it takes to get back into your dream state. Do it again. Find another picture that moves you. Write about it.

Do this process a number of times, till you have a bank of images. Say eight or ten. This will give you the flexibility you need to drop images in and out later, and will let you pick images that seem to have a common theme.

Action Steps:

1. Get into a semi-dream state.

2. Find an emotionally charged image.

3. Free associate round that image and write it up.

4. Repeat till you have 8-10 well developed images.

Time taken: 1-3 days.

Step 2: Find Your Hero And Villain

Somewhere in that mass of images you will have found the person you are most interested in. One person will keep tugging at you. The script will be their story. They are your protagonist, your lead character, your Hero.[3]

(I'm not using this word in the strictest sense. In my scripts the Hero doesn't have to be a good guy, just the guy that we are most interested in following – the guy whose struggle in which we are most invested, the guy the film is about.)

---

[3] People bang on and on about how you need to write reams about our characters, how you need to know everything about them, from the moment they were conceived, to what they liked for school dinner, to what they would give their mother for Christmas. Frankly, with all due respect for the acres of paper and thousand of hours that have been expended on this point, this is rubbish.

You don't need to write anything down about your characters. Maybe a sentence, to jog your memory. Not a bean more.

Oh, I used to. I used to pride myself on beautifully drawn character portraits that glowed on the page and made people go – 'wow, such interesting characters, you're so perceptive, how DO you do it...' The problem was that the minute I came to write the script I found those character biographies were redundant. In fact, more than that, they got in the way. By the end I'd look at what I had written down in the biog, and what I had ended up with in the script, and the gap was always profound.

First give them a name. Call them after someone you know. When you think of them in the story see the person you know playing the role.

As the story grows, they will separate off and acquire their own powerful personality, but for the moment, this nebulous cloud of emotions you are building about this character is pure gold.

Attack Your Hero

Now imagine something truly terrible that could happen to that person. What is the thing that, if they lost it, would scare them, or hurt them, the most.

Take your time over this – it determines everything about your screenplay. If you are writing an episode of a TV show you will be constrained by the world of that TV show – you can't really have a serious fear of murder in an episode of Friends. If you are writing a movie script you have to be guided by your own instincts a little more, but the same principle applies.

Whatever this terrible thing is will set up your world, and your genre. If, for example, your character would be most affected by losing their wife to an anonymous kidnapper, then you are probably going to be writing a thriller. If your character would be most affected by his television set breaking down, then you are possibly writing an episode of The Simpsons. Your character losing the chance to be with their soulmate, then you are writing romance. Etc.

Whatever this terrible thing is, one way or another, in the course of your story, this WILL happen to your character, at least temporarily.

Create Your Villain

Now, the next big job. Who did this terrible thing to your beloved Hero? Which person is so bad that they would deliberately strike at the very heart of your Hero to hurt them in this way?

This person is your <u>Antagonist, or Villain</u>. Do the same thing. Give them a name. Run around with them in your head. Get to know them. And don't write more than a sentence about them.

Single Most Important Guiding Principle

Your screenplay is the story of the battle between your Protagonist and your Antagonist.

Never lose sight of this.

Action Steps:

1. Find your hero.

2. Find your hero's worst nightmare.

3. Find your villain.

Time taken: 1-2 days.

Step 3: Find The Story Tent Poles

Now. Look at your list of images. Pick the <u>four</u> most interesting, vivid, the ones that you go WOW about whenever you remember them.

Put your Hero into those pictures. The job is to alter the picture so that in some way your Hero is doing something in each of these scenes. It's usually best to make it so that the thing that makes you go wow about the scene is something that actually happens to the Hero – or, far better, something your Hero is doing to someone else. These are going to be big scenes in your story.

Put these four scenes in ascending order. Smallest to biggest. Small and yet intriguing at the start, biggest and most dramatic at the end. Don't sweat it, don't worry about what is 'dramatic', or 'intriguing', just do it. Your instinct, trained by all the thousands of hours of watching TV and movies you have done, plus your own deep feelings about the scenes, will tell you in which order they should go.

The first three scenes should create a desire in your Hero – after each of these scenes your Hero should want to go and do something much more strongly than they did before they entered the scene. The fourth scene is going to be the ending of the story, so whatever the moment is, it should satisfy the desire that your hero has had throughout the script.

Let me put that more formally:

❖ The first, smallest event, creates a Desire in your Hero.

❖ The second and third events should modify and amplify that Desire so that your Hero feels it more powerfully, and is more motivated to fight the Villain.

❖ The fourth, largest event, is the payoff to that Desire, an event that brings the struggle for that Desire to a satisfying end.

You now have the basic tent poles of the very first version of your story.

The first event is where the story starts. The last, biggest event, is the climax of the story, the end of Act 3. The other two events are the ends of Act 1 and Act 2 respectively.[4]

You now have to build the story. Which means filling in the gaps between these poles. I'll cover that in Steps 6-12.

Remember, nothing is remotely permanent at this stage. As you go on you might very well swap poles

---

[4] There's a whole school of thought that says this kind of overt structuring is anti art and should never be mentioned in polite company, and certainly never allowed to influence the purity of the writer's thoughts. This is bullshit. It's perpetuated by the many inexperienced script editors and producers who have no idea about how to construct a story. It leads to rambling, flabby rubbish. People love structure. The whole story hangs off these moments, these tent poles, and you MUST have them.

There is another school of thought that says this structure is old fashioned, and out dated, and other more subtle structures should be operating within the script. Well, that's possibly very true, but the case has been overstated. I'll fill you in more about the only overlays you need to make on this basic structure in the Step called 'Beating It Out'.

out, replacing one or all of them with other events. All is possible. But always keep in mind that without four tent poles in place like this you don't have a story.

Action Steps:

1. Select the four most powerful images.
2. Put your hero into them.
3. Set them in ascending order.

Time taken: ½ day to 1 day.

Step 4: Research

So after you have completed the last action steps you should have the very first version of your story structure.

That means you now roughly know what the world is that you will be writing about.

Now you need to put those scenes aside and go out to research that world.

Make It Real, Make It Count

I don't mean wasting your time reading endless books about it, or finding obscure first hand conversational transcripts about it on the internet. I mean getting out into the real world, and talking to the people who you want to write about.

Get talking to as many people you can. Pull in favours, use friends of friends, make direct approaches, whatever works to get you in the same room as a couple of these people.

Don't think, "Oh, I can't do that, I'm far too shy, besides, isn't writing all about being inventive?" Think instead, "OK, so it's crucial, how do I do that?"

I've never written a good script about something I hadn't seen with my own eyes, and even more crucially, felt with my own emotions.

Avoid The Internet

The temptation is to lean back on the mass of material you can find on the internet, or in books.

If you look hard you can find first hand testimonies that can be shattering in their openness, technical details of how things work, floor plans, insights into the minds of killers, cops, lovers, psychics, seducers, mothers, grandfathers, all sorts.

I've been there, I know how tempting it is to just sit at your computer and read. The thing is that nothing works like getting out and getting into the places you are writing about, watching the people you are writing about, and talking to them about their lives.

Make the Familiar Strange

Even if you think you know the world you are writing about, go and do the research. The very fact you are there researching means you will look at the place, and what happens in it, with a far more objective eye, and you will notice quirks, interactions, emotions, that you have never seen before, that feel real, that get you away from cliché.

Why Research?

The real reason for me loving research is simple. It takes the real hard work out of writing a script.

Real life is endlessly surprising, endlessly refreshing, and will give you a mass of story material, most of which you would never have come up with on your own. To write powerfully about something you need that something to have hit you emotionally, to have hit you where it goes in deep so it can churn around in your subconscious. Talking to people face to face or seeing things actually happen has a habit of doing that. Getting your material out of history books, or off the internet, or from other second hand sources, will never have the same power. [5]

Opening The Doors

It's amazing how easy it is to get to people. Just ask. To get into institutions like the police, or the army, or the government, go to their press offices. Some of the time this is amazingly simple. You can be entirely straight, or you can invent whatever story you need.

I normally say that I am writing a proposal for a mass market TV show. That is usually true, but it doesn't have to be because they rarely check. (They have checked on the odd occasion, asking for a note on the TV/Film company's letterhead.

If they do that, and you can't muster a similar letter, then just say it's a speculative approach, you're a local writer, just looking for half an hour of their time, whenever they feel free enough to spare it. Play very humble, polite, genuine, and you'd be surprised how many times they will let you in.)

Once they open the doors, depending on how they feel about the media, and what they have to hide, the

---

[5] If you are gifted, prolific, and you have a mass of invention at your fingertips, so you only have to frown and ten stories pop into your mind, then don't think that lets you off the hook. You need to research even more than the rest of us – I've worked with writers like this, some of the most prolific storytellers in the UK, and their production rate is staggering. Yet frequently the screenplays are ungrounded, unreal, and not in a good way. Writers like this succeed because of the sheer momentum of their story telling, yet their stuff often has a fake feeling to it, and their very best work happens when they have taken the time to research the world they are writing about.

PR person will sometimes want to sit in on your interviews. This is research death, as whoever you are talking to will normally clam up tight.

I've found the best policy is to let this happen, and keep the interview short, treat it as a loss leader, and get the contact details of the people you are talking to. You can then arrange to meet up another time, without the inhibiting factor of the press person, and really fish for the grit.

If the press department won't let you in, because they got stitched up by the last TV company they did talk to, then you have to use your personal network. You know people, who know people, who know people. Put the word out. You'll find the contact you need in the end – and all it takes is one person involved in the world you are interested in to fling the door wide open.

Find The Right Source

The truth is that most people want the chance to tell you their story. The other, sadder, truth is that a lot of these people will be… shhh…. boring. They won't have much to tell you. Or what they do tell you sends you to sleep. Or what they do tell you sounds great at the time because you are excited by being in their world, but when you get home and actually write it up you realise it's about as exciting as a bowl of porridge.

You need people who have vivid stories to tell, and who are great at telling them. Try asking whoever is setting up the meeting to put you in touch with 'a real character'. Every place has one person who is famous for being slightly unusual, who knows all the gossip, or has a bit of an attitude – and they can be a great start. But you have to look around you and be prepared to dive after anyone if you get a whiff they are interesting.

One night I was out with the police, and I got lumbered in a car well away from any trouble with two very nice policemen who seemed to think that most people were basically OK and being in the police was fine and no, they really didn't have anything to complain about when it came to life.

Lovely guys, who took very good care of me, but I went home tearing my hair out. I'd been stitched up by one of the Inspectors on the relief, who didn't want me too close to anything too front line. He'd found the two most placid guys in the station, who were famous for their desire for an easy life, and told them to stay out of trouble for the evening.

Luckily I had two night's access booked. Next night I concocted a broken down train so that I arrived an hour later, at shift handover time. All the guy who had assigned me the previous night could do was introduce me and head off home. I got someone else to look after me for the evening. Who had a completely different idea about liaison with writers, and put me in the fastest car at the station, so I spent the evening zooming backwards and forwards to different incidents, all the time besieged by the contained rage of the guy behind the wheel who hated the public, was having a passionate affair with three women at the police station, and would die for his mates. Guess which evening contributed more to the script I was writing?

Researching Sci Fi, and Historical Drama

OK, so what if you're writing a Science Fiction screenplay about the invasion of Planet Blorax by the Niddons? Well, get in touch with the army. Talk to a real soldier or two. Find out how they think. Find out what real soldiers feel about real armies, and battles in history, especially in wars with vastly different cultures. Take the sensibility you discover and play with it till it feels alien. But never lose touch with the reality.

What about the ancient Romans? They're all dead. Well, of course, but human nature, and human society, isn't that different. (Just read Petronius if you doubt that.) So, if you're writing about the Senate, go talk to your local council members and get them to talk about what really goes on in election campaigns. If you are talking about Roman orgies, go find a local brothel and see if you can't find a way of hanging out there for a day or two. (Unsavoury advice? Yeah, well, maybe, but you need reality in your script.)

How Long To Research?

When I started out I used to worry about how long this phase should be. There are two situations I can think of:

If you are working for a deadline, you have limited time for this. If I'm doing a TV show with all the pressures, then I will usually only take a week to do this. (By which I mean I do nothing other than explore the world I want to write about: no writing, no story-lining, just soaking stuff up.)

If I am writing something more open ended, where there is no shooting date set, then I will take as long as I need. The worry was always that I was procrastinating, putting off the hard business of writing by just socialising – in fact it doesn't work like that.

There will come a point where you will feel like your head is bursting with stuff you know about this world, and you are desperate to get some of it down on

26

paper. That's how you know it's time to end the research phase and start writing.

Your only problem (and it's not really a problem, because you will quickly have so much material) will be restricting your selection to just a handful of story ideas/characters/events from a tremendous mass of vivid events and anecdotes.

The Best Kind Of Notes

One other thing is that I rarely take detailed notes or use Dictaphones when I am actually interviewing people – I find that that leads to me taking down too much detail. Just headline sentences will do.

If something is interesting, and dramatically powerful enough to use in your story, then you WILL remember it, no problem. I do however spend an hour or two at the end of the day, or perhaps the next morning, writing up what I can remember about what I learned in that day. And do make sure you write down any colourful phrases you have heard. They are gold when it comes to writing your dialogue.

Those notes, slightly abstracted as they are, tend to give you great ideas for stories when you look back on them, and always act to drag your head back into the world if you are in danger of forgetting what is like to be there with those people.

Action Steps:

1.   Get out and into the world of your story.

2.   Find people in this world who have an attitude about the world.

3.   Hang out with them.

4.   Keep summary notes at the end of each day.

Time taken: 1 week / open ended.

Step 5: Check Your Tent Poles

This is a small, but crucial step.

After you have come back from your research phase, your head will be spinning with what you have seen, and your subconscious will be brimming with story ideas.

Take the time to go over the tent poles you selected in Step 3. It's likely that what seemed compelling when you knew nothing about the world now seems slightly uninteresting. You should take the time to make sure that the four images you want to go forward with are the strongest in your arsenal.

Action Steps:

1. Check you have selected the most powerful images for your four most pivotal scenes.

Time taken: ½ to 1 day.

The Beat Sheet

So. This is where it gets serious. The first thing to say is, don't ever give up. After giving it your very best shot and then some, if you feel you can't do it, and you'll never be a writer and who were you to imagine you had anything worth saying, well, just join the club. I don't know any successful writer who doesn't entertain those thoughts, and usually in this stage.

And it's not just the writer. If you're working with a producer, or a story editor (a script editor in the UK) or other writers, you will ALL find it hard.

That old line about 'writing is easy, you just stare at a piece of paper till your forehead bleeds' is never truer than at this point.

Just know it's going to be hard, know it will defeat you at first - and then keep on doggedly pushing till you break through. You WILL do it. It just may take days, or weeks. Please don't think that, because you have just spent a couple of hour's thought when nothing inspired happened, that you are not cut out to be a writer. It takes much, much more effort than that, and that is perfectly normal!

This IS A Formula, Right?

Now. I'm about to tell you the story shape I use. I'm about to tell you how to write the sort of story that people always want to read.

PLEASE don't write to me and tell me that you can't dictate stories in this way, that they should be unique, original, one offs. Or ask how dare I dictate something that should never be dictated. Or inform me that what I am recommending will lead to dry, dull, formulaic stories that will bore an audience rigid.

I know that's what a lot of people believe.

I repeat, <u>I know that's what a lot of people believe</u>!

But I also know that this particular story shape creates stories that people read, and enjoy, and HIRE YOU from.

Once you're in a position of strength, once you have penetrated the citadel, well, then you can experiment with new ways of working.

But I tell you, be careful even then. I'm well within the citadel, and I find this story shape does me just fine.

If you use this story shape you will have a far greater chance of working as a writer.

And that IS what you want, isn't it?

What Is A Beat Sheet?

So. The ultimate goal at this point is to come up with a 'Beat Sheet'.

This is a list of single sentences. Perhaps 50-70 for an hour of television, perhaps 90-120 for a typical movie script. Each of these sentences summarises an event, or "beat", in your story. When you read the entire list of sentences in sequence you will be able to play the whole film in your head more or less as it will happen on screen.

By the time you finish, this list of sentences should naturally divide into three big chunks. These are usually called Act One, Act Two and Act Three. Each of these chunks has different components, and each component should be present, in roughly the right place.

But getting to that point is a long way off. And it can be a very rocky road.

The point of this long section, the heart of the book, is that I'm going to take you through the whole thing, give you a set of tools, show you exactly what you need to know to get there.

For me the act of writing is a matter of bouncing around between four tools until I get to the magic place of having a completed Beat Sheet.

Four Crucial Tools

The tools are:

❖ Finding your 'Logline'.

❖ The procedure I call 'Beating It Out'.

❖ The 'Minor Character Stories'.

❖ The 'Hero Design Sheet'.

Now, there is nothing linear about these tools. You don't use them in any particular order.

The idea is that you start somewhere, with one of the tools. You play with that a while, then take whatever you have created there, and work on one of the other tools. Taking the results of that, you can either go back to the first tool, or to a third. And so on.

So, maybe you start with some of the story beats in Beating it Out. Whatever you create on the Beat Sheet might then feed into your thinking about your Hero, which then could feed back into your Beat Sheet, and maybe over to your Minor Character Stories - which influences what you are thinking about your Logline, which then perhaps bounces back to the Hero Design Sheet again, in an organic process of growth which may seem like knitting water at first but will, I guarantee, eventually settle down.

I can't tell you exactly when to switch activities – I do it differently every time, and it really is a matter for your instincts. All I can say is that when you feel you've hit a brick wall, that you've run dry on inspiration, then go to one of the other tools and see how that plays out.

If you are working on Beat It Out, there will come a point when you have used all the good images you thought of in Step 1, plugged them all in, found glaring gaps in the beat sheet, run out of inspiration, run out of steam, all your ideas seem trite, and clichéd, and you wish you'd taken up another easier vocation like herding cats or being a test pilot.

That's when you can stop trying to Beat It Out for a while and go to play around with your other tools.

The one crucial thing to remember is the Beat Sheet, the Hero Design Sheet, the Minor Character Design Sheet, and the Logline should all be consistent with each other at the end of the Story Design Process, before you start writing scenes and dialogue.

Time spent on any of the four tools is time well spent. Just remember that your Beat Sheet is your ultimate road map. Bounce between it and other pages of notes, and diagrams, and documents, but the ever more completed Beat Sheet is the Master Document. You will measure your progress by how full this is and how well it reads.

So let's have a look at the tools:

Step 6: Finding Your Logline

This isn't a logline in the traditional sense of a hot and enticing sentence that will sell your story to every studio in Hollywood. The way I use logline is to indicate a sentence that pins down the absolute content of your story in the most concise form possible.

If you've read any other books about screenwriting you will probably recognise this idea. But most other books say you need to decide what's in this sentence up front. From years of experience, I think this is rubbish.

Every big discovery you make about your story will have an impact on your logline. Over the course of you completing your beat sheet you will find your logline changes like the wind.

But you should constantly be thinking about it, always have it in the back of your mind. And try to keep it up to date, so that it represents the current state of your thinking about your story.

So what is it?

Simple. It's a sentence in this format:

"In struggling to Do X, Person Y reaches the new emotional state Z."

"In struggling to defeat Darth Vader, Luke Skywalker, a simple farm hand from a rural backwater, becomes a great Jedi Knight." *Star Wars*

"In struggling to defeat Le Chiffre, James Bond, an already hard nosed British Secret Service Agent, has his heart broken and becomes a hardened killing machine." *Casino Royale*

"In struggling to regain his former love Ilsa, Rick, a selfish and cold hearted bartender, rediscovers what it means to have Heart." *Casablanca*

Action Steps:

1. Create your first version of your Logline.

Time taken: 5 mins – 1 hour, but ongoing.

Step 7: Beating It Out - Act 1

The second tool is the process of beating out your 3 Act Structure, the foundation of your screenplay.

Act 1 is roughly the first 25% of your story. (That means it's perhaps 15 sentences of a 60 beat TV hour beat sheet, perhaps 25 sentences of a 100 beat movie beat sheet.)

Act 2 is the middle 50% of your story (maybe 30 sentences of a TV hour beat sheet, and 50 sentences of a movie beat sheet) and Act 3 is the last 25% of your story (15 and 25 sentences again.)

The first thing is to say never get hung up on those precise numbers, they're just there as guides. When I first started out I was always sure to hit them precisely; now I play much more freely with them. (If they are wildly out, like, say, you have an Act 1 of 7 beats, then you should take a closer look at what's going on with the structure – you might well have a problem worth fixing.)

So let's take the first big chunk of the story and get going.

You create your Act 1 by dramatising this very particular setup:

"My hero/heroine is such and such a person, living in such and such a situation, with an everyday <u>Familiar Problem</u> that he or she knows about and such and such a psychological need that he or she isn't aware of.

In the course of a normal day for them they take their usual steps to tackle their familiar problem when something unusual

37

happens, and creates a new need for them to solve this Unusual Problem. (This need usually takes the shape of a question in their head.) They should pretty well drop else everything they are doing at this point, and work on answering this question.

After a bit of a struggle they get to a point where they get their answers, or they get their need satisfied, only to find out that in accomplishing this they have opened up a whole new, and much, much bigger problem

This is the end of Act 1."

Let's break that down into what's needed. You have to:

1. Show us your Hero, show us what kind of a person they are, and their normal everyday life.

2. Show us how they have a Familiar Problem.

3. Show them taking steps to solve their Familiar Problem.

4. Show how, somewhere along the line, they will encounter an unusual event which produces their Unusual Problem.

5. This unusual event is called the Inciting Incident, and this is a crucial screenwriting concept. It can be the tiniest thing, but it should have the potential to turn the Protagonist's life upside down, and to create a situation that will last till the end of the screenplay. When you are looking for this incident, you need to find the event that will eventually lead your hero into the most difficult struggle of their life.

6. Show the Hero taking steps to solve the Unusual Problem

7. Show how they finally get to solve their Unusual Problem.

8. Out of the frying pan, into the fire. Show how they realise they now have an utterly unexpected, horrifyingly urgent, Massive Problem. This realisation concludes Act 1.

As a writer you now have the problem of working out how to dramatise these steps. You should first of all re-read the list of scenes and vivid images you created in Step 1. Make sure they are all fresh in your mind – you could well find yourself slotting one or several of them into place in the course of beating out the story.

Example Story Idea

Start at the beginning. Let's run with a very simple story idea. Nothing very interesting in the wider scheme of things, no award winning or radical new piece here, just a simple narrative that can be used to illustrate how the system works:

Imagine your brainstorming has left you with a hero, and a handful of scenes.

You have decided to call your hero 'Laura', after a friend you had at school, who just didn't seem worldly enough to exist in this life.

Flying in the face of conventional screenwriting wisdom, you have decided to avoid all the cool guys you knew and you have picked this friend who you loved, because at some instinctive level you are fascinated by her, and think there is something to say about her.

When you think back to this girl you knew at school your overriding memory is of desperately wanting her to look after herself, but her being so innocent, or such a loser, that bad things always seemed to happen to her.

The fact you feel an emotion like this is very important – you need to love your protagonist, man or woman. You need to care for them deeply, you need to feel big compassion for their situation. You are going to make bad things happen to them, and you need to care what happens, so that you can make your audience care what happens. You will need them to win at the end, most definitely, so they will have to be capable of learning deep and powerful things about themselves in your story. But that's a long way off, so to begin with just make sure you love some aspect of them.

In the case of Laura, you have decided that the worst thing that could happen to her is a sustained threat of violence by someone much physically stronger than her. When you think back to the Laura you knew at school you remember her very law abiding nature and her deep trust of authority figures. You decide therefore it should be someone she trusts as an authority figure and protector who should betray her like this. Because they are the villain you need to give them a name that has unpleasant connotations for you, so they occupy the right emotional place in your mind.

Then let's just imagine two of your ten or twelve scenes, both the pictures, and the reason the pictures might be appealing to you. You've done the work, and put Laura into both of the scenes.

The first image, your first tent pole, was a woman finding what looks like an innocent box in the back of an office cupboard. You as the writer know this box contains something that will blow her life apart – yet it looks so innocuous.

You find this a very powerful idea – the theme of danger rumbling just under the surface of an everyday environment seems fascinating. You love that moment at which Laura reaches for the box, and opens it. Pandora's box is a timeless theme – if only Laura had left it alone. It's also a classic opening for a story – so let's treat it as our inciting incident.

Your subconscious has clearly already been running with your theme of violent attack, because in another of your brainstorming moments you saw the second image: a dark, rainy street, and a very ordinary looking woman running into a threat of deadly violence from a man who should be a protector. Perhaps he is even wearing the uniform of a protector.

You find that a very charged situation. You are fascinated by the idea of how a person utterly ill-equipped for the intrusion of violence into their life like Laura might handle it. To you this scene feels emotionally bigger than the previous idea, so it should probably be later. For the moment you decide to experiment with it being your second tent pole, the end of Act 1.

Second Software Tool

Now you need your second software tool. Not a screenwriting package, but a spreadsheet. I use Excel, but it really doesn't matter which. If you are strapped for cash, Google provide a free spreadsheet at docs.google.com. Or, once again, try OpenOffice.org.

You're not interested in the calculation facilities – you're interested in the neat way you can cut and paste cells, and selections of cells. You've probably heard about all those whiteboards full of story beats, or, going back a while, index cards pinned to a huge board – well, a spreadsheet lets you do all of this on your computer screen and is far easier to work with.

Your beat sheet is a spreadsheet of all the story beats, arranged by character.

Go back to your two scenes. Enter them into the spreadsheet like this:

	A	B	C
1		**LAURA**	**VILLAIN**
2			
3			
4			
5			
6			
7			
8	**Inciting Incident**	*Find and open box*	
9			
10			
11			
12			
13			
14	**End of Act 1**	Gets threat from Tony	Threatens Laura

Figure 1: Act 1, first few beats charted.

You fill in the one beat you know about the villain at the same time.

It certainly seems to make sense to try out the threatening uniformed man as the Villain.

You have decided to call him Tony, after a guy you knew who was the office bully. You find it a lot harder to love this person, but even then, by stretching your imagination, you can empathise with him.

In real life Tony was the kind of guy who desperately wants to be accepted, but due to self esteem problems can't believe that people would ever really like him, and he falls for aggressive and increasingly desperate ways of proving how likeable he is.

42

The fact that you understand his motivation like this is useful – it means you can find it within yourself to care for him, which will show in all sorts of subtle ways as you build your story.

Note something important here. In your story you see the antagonist as a near supernaturally empowered stalker, not Freddie Krueger, but in that direction, and Tony was just a normal guy, so the parallels don't run too far.

But what is important is the seed – given that most of us aren't really acquainted with truly evil people, as a writer you are probably going to have to extrapolate from what you know. Your workmate Tony wasn't a bad guy because he wanted to be loved. He was a bad guy because he was prepared to use a lot of cruelty to get what he wanted. You are just going to take these traits and amplify them.

Create Your Battle

So, you have your two characters. What has been going on between them? How do we connect the two scenes?

Ask yourself 'Who Is My Hero'? That is: what is her world in my story?

The real Laura was a meek and mild bank clerk the last time you heard of her, so you decide your fictional Laura is the kind of girl to work in an office, and that she's also the kind of girl to have a crush on someone and do nothing about it.

So maybe an average sort of problem for her could be that some chance to get close to her crush arises. Maybe she gets an invite to a party to which this crush will be going. And maybe it's that evening, and maybe she hasn't got anything to wear.

43

So that could be her Familiar Problem. A nice, normal problem, coming out of her everyday life.

Note that story is your character taking steps to get the things they want. Nothing more, nothing less.

So to find Laura's story we need to work out what steps she would take to solve her problem.

You think she might decide to leave early so she can get to the shops and get herself something to wear before they close. Sounds like a plan.

Obstacles And Comebacks

Important note. Never, ever allow your characters to go very far without obstacles. Conflict is the life blood of a story. The minute Conflict goes off screen is the minute you start to lose your audience.

You should always be going from Obstacle, to Comeback, to Obstacle, to Comeback.

So Laura needs an obstacle, pretty quick.

Let's decide her boss is an unreasonable sort, but Laura is keen to get his agreement, so she butts into a meeting he is having with Tony, the firm's security guard. When Laura comes in she hears Tony tell the Boss that the CCTV security system in the building has failed and will cost a couple of thousand to repair. This is giving the boss considerable indigestion of the wallet. Laura knows this is a danger sign, but presses ahead. Asks if she can leave early. Boss blows up, and tells her no way she can leave early. In fact today he wants some extra work out of her and so she has to stay at work till late.

This is her first Obstacle. She took steps to get her goal – which was to solve her Familiar Problem, and got blocked.

And this is where Laura has to reach inside herself to overcome this obstacle. She needs a Comeback. You have to find a way for her to do this and remain true to herself.

So at this point you decide that Laura is actually more desperate than you had first imagined. She is SO into her crush, she is prepared to take a risk. She really, really wants to look good at the party. So her Comeback is she decides to sneak out early and get down to the shops despite what her boss had said.

(Notice how her taking this action reveals some of her character. She is more of a risk taker than you first thought. That's all you have to reveal thought processes on screen – the choices made by your characters.)

This generates a bit more story for you. To get out of work this early she will have to accomplish a couple of things.

❖ She will have to offload her work onto her fellow employees

❖ And she will have to sneak out the building without being seen.

These are the steps to solve her Familiar Problem, and they give us more story material.

Her plan starts off fine. Though Greg her workmate grumbles, he agrees to help her. (This is all good and useful stuff – it shows us what kind of woman Laura is perceived to be – i.e. she has friends - and establishes characters who may or may not come in useful later on)

So it's all going well. Therefore it must be just about time for another Obstacle: Sneaking out of the office on her way to the shops she sees the boss ahead of her, closing fast. She has her coat on, is carrying her bag, it's obvious she's leaving the office. If he sees her after what he told her she is in big trouble.

Her Comeback is to go and slip through a convenient door and hide in the big stock room.

Obstacle: the boss is actually coming to the stock room.

Comeback: She shrinks into a nook in the very back of the room. The boss comes into the cupboard, and starts rummaging around pulling stuff off the shelves in front of her.

Obstacle: She trips over a box.

Comeback: Luckily the boss doesn't hear her.

Obstacle: She should be hiding but she sees the box, can't resist opening it. Inside the box is a whole host of missing personal property, all stolen from the desks around the building.

Obstacle: The boss catches her, apparently red handed.

So now we have got to her Unusual Problem. Laura protests her innocence, but now the Boss thinks she is the thief. And he wants her out.

This even is your Inciting Incident. It puts Laura in a very, very unusual place. Thematically it makes her enter the world of criminality, which is the world of the final screenplay. Practically, in story terms, she has to start taking unusual steps to sort this situation out. It is the first link in a chain of increasingly dramatic cause and effect that will last for the rest of the story.

Comeback: She protests, and in the light of there being no real evidence (the broken CCTV cameras) she is allowed to stay at work. But the boss is on her case.

Comeback: She decides to stake out the office after hours. And indeed this does solve the Unusual Problem. She sees Tony stealing a laptop. She pulls out her digital camera, and takes photos of him in the act.

Comeback: She shows the photos to the boss.

Comeback: The boss sacks Tony.[6] Co-workers celebrate even more when it turns out Tony has a big criminal record.

And then we get to the final scene in the act. Which always has to be an 'Out of the frying pan, into the fire' moment, the biggest obstacle of all so far, which must give your Hero a Massive New Problem. If you get this right your audience will be riveted to their seats, desperate to find out what happens to the character they have invested in.

We've got to our End of Act 1 beat: the image you've had in your head from the beginning – vulnerable woman accosted by man who should be protector:

So:

Obstacle: leaving work Laura is hurrying along a rainy street when she realises she is being followed. It's. Tony. He's lost his job, and the police are going to charge him. He tells her from now on she needs to better watch her back. He's going to ruin her life.

End of Act 1.

---

[6] Note how it's perfectly fine to have more than one Comeback, or Obstacle in a row. All it means is that when the next switch comes it has to be slightly bigger.

Charting The Beats

The first thing to say is that this isn't a story that will ever light anyone's fire, but we know that. The point is it shows you how the system works.

So now you need to turning each of these beats into a sentence, and put them into the spreadsheet. You will end up with something like the situation opposite.

Now you have completed charting Act 1.

Action Steps:

Produce a spread sheet charting the following beats:

1. Show us your Hero, what kind of a person they are, and their everyday life. (One or more beats)

2. They discover a Familiar Problem(s). (Single beat)

3. Steps they take to solve their Familiar Problem. (One or more beats.)

4. Inciting Incident to create their Unusual Problem. (A single beat)

5. Steps they take in which they try to solve their Unusual Problem. (One or more beats.)

6. They finally solve their Unusual Problem. (Single beat)

7. Out of the frying pan, into the fire. They discover their Massive Problem. (Single Beat)

Time taken: ½ day – 2 days initially, but ongoing till the end.

	A	B	C	D
1		**LAURA**	**VILLAIN**	**GREG**
2		Laura's confidence crumbles as her crush walks past		Jokes with Laura re. her lack of dating confidence
3		Hears he will be at the party tonight		
4		Angles for invite, gets it, but has nothing to wear		
5		Boss refuses to let her leave early	tells boss CCTV system is kaput	
6		She decides to go anyway, offloads her work		Agrees to help Laura by taking her work on
7		Sees boss ahead of her, hides in cupboard		
8	**Inciting Incident**	*Find and open box*		
9		Boss wants to suspend her, she argues and keeps job		
10		Her friends points out she has to catch real thief		tells Laura she has to catch real thief
11		She stakes out office, catches Tony in act	Gets caught stealing	
12		Boss sacks Tony	gets sacked	
13		Friends pleased when other stolen items returned		gets his stolen laptop back
14	**End of Act 1**	Gets threat from Tony	threatens Laura	

Figure 2: Act 1 beats charted

49

Step 8: Beating It Out – Act 2

Sadly there is no simple template for Act 2 like the one we used for Act 1. The battle becomes much more about taking the story and running with it wherever it takes you, and things do get much more fluid.

You will of course constantly create Obstacle and Comeback, just like before, and make sure they get bigger and bigger throughout the act.

And, just like you had to hit an Inciting Incident, and End of Act 1, there are a set of other obligatory beats you must cover in Act 2 and 3.

I'll cover these obligatory beats in the order I normally get to them. (I wouldn't worry TOO much about sticking to this order, but I have found this does work well for me.)

Hero's Plan

The first thing is that very near to the start of Act 2 you will create a beat in which you lay out the course of action your Hero thinks he will follow in order to defeat the Villain.

Maybe in our story above we get the idea that Laura, being the law abiding woman she is, is going to trust other authority figures to defend her.

Villain's Plan

Some time soon after telling us how the Hero is going to work towards victory you need to do the same thing with the Villain. We need to see a beat where we understand fully the path they intend to take to bring the Hero to physical/moral/emotional destruction.

I'm not saying here that you should get the Villain, or the Hero for that matter, talking his plan through with a cohort – it's way better if the plan is implicit in the actions of the Villain. So the way the Villain responds to the Hero's plan should make us think – 'ohhh, they've blocked our Hero in their path, and the fact that they have done it in this way means that they will be doing this in future...'

The Villain's plan must also be long term, with various steps that need executing, so that the Hero and the Villain can tussle.

In the example story Tony might break into Laura's home and shred all her childhood photos. This would be a very personal attack, leading Laura to realise his plan to vandalise and bring down every part of her life.

Note that it is not enough for the Villain's plan to be simply 'respond to each move the Hero makes and defeat them'. They must have a scheme they are constantly chasing themselves. That allows you to have an ebb and flow situation: sequences of beats where the Hero is chasing their plan, and the Villain is on the back foot, and merely responding, and then other sequences of beats where the Villain is chasing their plan and the Hero is frantically trying to stop him.

Hero and Villain Execute Their Plans

Having got these two plans up and visible, having set out your stall for the audience in this way, you can then go onto building the bulk of Act 2. In the early stages this should be basically a set of beats in which the Hero and the Villain slug it out, trading blows, and escalating their plans and the dramatic heat. Each step by the hero to get what they want must be countered by an even bigger blow by the antagonist. This battle of wits and energies makes up the bulk of Act 2.

What happens in this phase is up to you. But it's crucial that the sense should soon emerge that the Hero is getting beaten. That whatever they do, the Villain is more resourceful, more canny, stronger, than them. This should start to press your Hero into a corner.

Hero Goes Bad

At which point you get to the next obligatory beat. At the point where they seem to be running out of options, your Hero must resort to acting immorally, according to their own terms.

In the story above, this could be the point at which a very, very scared Laura goes to some local criminals, and pays for some professionals to frighten Tony off.

Or maybe, depending how far down the line with her you have got, you find a way of her striking back against Tony in a more personal way – maybe she befriends Tony's mother and feeds her damaging information about her son. Whatever. The point is that the Hero has been driven to previously unimaginable actions by the battle with the villain.

This amended plan should only come after all their normal resources have failed, and is a way that you escalate the story.

Think about it. It would cost a person to act against their best held principles; the fact that they are having to do so at this point in your story means that they are getting into serious trouble – which is great for the drama.

Warning Shot

This should lead pretty quickly to the next obligatory beat: a moment where our Hero gets a verbal attack, a warning shot that they are acting immorally, from one of the characters that is on their side. They must reject this warning, and continue down the path they are travelling, into acts of deeper immorality.

This beat, and their reaction to it, marks a significant point in their journey. It shows how far they have gone – and they fact that they reject this call for 'good' behaviour will withdraw their normal sphere of support, isolating them in the world, increasing the pressure on them – and, hopefully, making us feel for them even more.

Total Defeat

Then you get to the end of Act 2. There are two huge obligatory beats which have to happen here: the moment of Total Defeat, and the moment of the Escape Hatch.

The Total Defeat is the point at which the Hero is apparently defeated. All their plans have failed. They have no resources left. If they have friends left then they have all been defeated. All hope is lost for them. They have lost all they were fighting for, and the Villain is just about to achieve his terrible victory.

The Escape Hatch

And then, probably in the same scene, or very quickly after, you open the Escape Hatch. The Hero gets some information at this point that they and the audience had no idea of until now. Somewhere in this information is the escape hatch. Somewhere in this information are the seeds of one last ditch plan. One last action they can take, which can lead to the most desperate plan of all. This propels the Hero on into Act 3 like they are on rocket fuel.

And that is the end of Act 2.

The figure on the following page illustrates the sort of thing you are building.

Action Steps:

1. Complete your spreadsheet with Act 2 beats.

Time taken: 1 day to 1 month. Ongoing.

	LAURA	VILLAIN	GREG
1			
16 ACT 2			
17 Battle beats...			
18 Battle beats...			
19 etc...			
20 Hero's Plan	Laura gets her big plan.		
21 Battle beats...	Laura does step one of her plan		Helps Laura out
22 etc...			
23 Villain's Plan	Tony defeats that step easily, and in doing so reveals his own plan	Tony retaliates - we see his plan	
24 Battle beats...	Laura regroups, fights		
25 Battle beats...	Tony beats her	Tony beats Laura	
26 Battle beats...	Laura fights harder		
27 Battle beats...	Tony raises his game, defeats Laura easily		
28 *Until...*	This goes on until...		
29 Hero goes bad	Laura hires contract killer		
30 Battle beats...			
31 Battle beats...			Find out she's hiring a killer
32 Warning Shot	Greg tells Laura she is out of order		Pleads with her to walk away
33 Battle beats...			
34 Total Defeat	Tony defeats contract killer, traps Laura		
35 Escape Hatch			
36 END OF ACT 2			

Figure 3: Act 2 beats charted

56

Step 9: Beating It Out – Act 3

So now we are into Act 3. The Hero breaks out of the clutches of the Villain, and they resume their battle. Move, counter move, blow, counter move, the stakes the highest they have ever been.

Brush With Death

At some point soon you get the Brush With Death. If anyone's read *The Hero With 1,000 Faces* by Joseph Campbell you will recognise this concept. He calls it 'The Belly of the Whale."

Many of the thousands of writer's handbooks around also mention this idea – and that's because it works. It sounds a little abstract, a little metaphysical, but trust me, if you can get this idea into your drama, around this place in your story, you are really getting somewhere.

The basic point is that the Hero has a moment where they recognise their own mortality. A moment where, in some subtle way, they realise that the universe is a big and powerful place, and they are small and mortal within it.

Try and find a location for this that in some way constricts the hero. A small, confined place where the Hero can experience desperate isolation.

The point is that this is the moment the Hero truly discovers his ultimate ability. You know when you've got it right when you can look at the moment and see it as a moment of enlightenment for the Hero, after which nothing – even death – can stop them.

Final Showdown

The next Obligatory Beat is a face to face battle between the Hero and the Villain. This is the scene the whole script has been waiting for. It's the moment they both meet, both tooled up, both aware they are fighting the fight of their lives.

You <u>must</u> dramatise: show don't tell. If the mechanics of the story you are telling allows it they should really meet face to face – and it is <u>critical</u> that this is a visually led, rather than dialogue heavy, scene.

Your Hero should win this battle, and get what he has been chasing all the way through the script. That's because you will get more audience satisfaction, and more future commissions, if you have a happy ending. Seriously.

I know what you are thinking – "but life doesn't have happy endings!" Well, maybe. But I'll just remind you, you aren't living life in this script, this script doesn't exist to help you work out metaphysical anxieties of your own (well, not primarily anyway). In this script your primary job is to entertain an audience, and most audiences tend to prefer happy endings. [7]

I don't want to labour this point because of all the misguided convictions held by new writers (including me, once upon a time) their belief in their god-given right to a downbeat ending is held most dear – I'll just warn you that if there is any advice you follow out of this book, then 'Hero Beats Villain' is up with the best.

---

[7] An audience craves visceral satisfaction at the end of the story and there are few things more visceral than seeing your team win!

Hero's Revelation

Somewhere around this time, during the battle, possibly just after it, there are two more Obligatory Beats; beats which must occur close together.

Firstly, the Hero must have a revelation about themselves. They should realise they have come to a new place in their lives, which has changed them. They should realise that when the story started they had a strong belief about themselves and the world that was wrong, and what has happened to them in the course of the story has made them realise this, changing them forever. (And, yes, if you are telling any story worth telling, that word 'forever' is very important.)

This leads to the penultimate Obligatory Beat:

The Hero's Choice

To get this right you need to have been working on the Hero Design Sheet. But basically the two poles of this choice underpin a conflicting Desire and Need that have been active in the Hero all the way through the script. Each pole should stand for a set of values and a way of living.

And – this is crucial – each pole of this choice must be seen as equally desirable by the Hero.

The action they take to resolve this choice (and it really must be a physical action, a move that we can actually SEE on screen – i.e., once again, whatever you do you mustn't do this in dialogue) nails the story once and for all.

If you can integrate this beat into the actual Final Showdown, and make it the means by which the Hero defeats the Villain, then you have done supremely well. If you can't, well, so long as it

59

happens around the same time then you will get much of the benefit.

Actually, it's impossible to overstate the importance of these two beats – if your Hero can't grow in this way your script will feel like a comic book.

If these two beats aren't present at the end of your script your story will feel flat, dull, and your audience will walk away with the disappointed sense of 'So What?' [8]

It's possible, just about, to start writing your script without being too clear on some of the other Obligatory Beats, but you MUST KNOW the contents of your Hero's Choice before you begin writing scenes and dialogue.

See the Hero Design Sheet section below for hard information on how to design this choice.

Coda

And finally, though after this Battle and Revelation, you really want to get out of the script as fast as you can, you need to put in one last Obligatory Beat, the Coda.

This is the beat in which you allow the fuss you've created to settle, the beat in which the audience catches their breath, and the beat in which you show how life will be for the Hero from now on after all they have done.

It allows the audience a moment to catch their breath, absorb what has happened, and feel good about how the story has ended.

---

[8] If you ever get as far as getting an audience! I say that because if these beats aren't present in your script in a way that feels earned, then it's unlikely that your script will ever get made.

	A	B	C	D
1		LAURA	VILLAIN	GREG
38	ACT 3			
39	Final struggle beats...			
40	**Brush with Death**	Laura is held, imprisoned somehow		
41	Final struggle beats...			
42	Final struggle beats...			
43	Final showdown	Laura defeats Tony		
44	**Hero's revelation**			
45	**Coda**	Show how Laura is now living in a better world - her struggle with Tony healed her inner turmoil		

Figure 4: Act 3 Beats charted

Note: You can have as many Introductory Beats, Battle Beats, and Final Struggle Beats as you feel you need, so long as you stick more or less to the 25%, 50% and 25% ration between Acts 1, 2 and 3.

Action Steps

Complete your spreadsheet with the Act 3 beats:

Time taken: 1 day to 1 month. Ongoing.

Step 10: Minor Character Stories

This is your third Tool - a small, but lethal weapon.

First of all, you have probably noticed that all the characters you are interested in should get their own column in the Beat Sheet.

Your other characters need story. It sounds obvious, but so many writers neglect this it isn't funny. You can get away with characters who don't go anywhere, who exist only to feed your hero, but your story will be SO much more rich and appealing if everyone in the script has a little arc.

The golden rule is if characters are in the same scene, then their beats should be on the same row of the spreadsheet. If they are in a scene on their own, then they get their own row, as shown in the next figure.

This may seem like duplication, but it really helps – if you can chart out every scene that every character is in, *from their viewpoint*, so you know what the events of that scene mean to that individual character, you are far more likely to give them a decent story.

These stories don't have to be nearly so fully realised as the story for your Hero (no need at all to go through all those obligatory beats, or even the tent poles) but for every character who has a decent sized speaking part in your script try to find at least three moments – a beginning moment, a middle moment, and an end moment. (And make sure the end moment leaves them in a different emotional place to where they started!)

LAURA	VILLAIN	GREG	
Goes to a party with her friends		Goes to party	
		Goes back to office	
Goes home	Follows Laura home		
		Falls asleep in office	
Finds Tony breaking into her house	Breaks into Laura's house		

Figure 5: Laying Out Character Beats

Action Steps

1. Make sure that the minor characters have their own stories.

Time taken: Ongoing throughout

Step 11: Character Design Sheets

Your fourth Tool has two aspects – designing your Hero, and designing your other characters.

Hero Design Sheet

Use this exercise to feed into the Hero's Revelation / Hero's Choice Obligatory Beats above.

It is an exercise you should complete at some point before you sign off the Beat Sheet. I find it pointless doing it too early, too close to when you start thinking about the story; and equally pointless doing it very late in the day when you have got a very solid storyline. You should come and have a go at these questions at some time when you run out of steam on the Beat Sheet.

I want to take you back to first principles for a moment, and remind you that the classic definition of Drama (and the most workable definition of Drama I have ever found) is 'Character in Conflict'.

The very essence of a dramatic hero is a Hero who is torn in two, and therefore the very end of your story contains a beat called the Hero's Choice.

This is the climax of the whole story, the point at which you get the most drama possible by putting your hero, a character we have loved and suffered with through all the battles of the preceding story, into a place where they are torn in half by the two equally powerful – and utterly opposing – desires they have carried throughout the whole story.

65

But how do we get that much drama? How do we get that character torn in two?

Simple. We design it at the outset. Before you ever write a word of dialogue you will have written down phrases for the following eight items:

1. Hero's Desire

Something the Hero *wants* very powerfully at the conscious level. A desire that sparks from the inciting incident in some way. A desire that, in the getting, will constantly force the character to act against the things their Need makes them want. It's the Holy Grail, to Catch the Murderer, to Win the Big Fight.

The Desire is the thing that the Villain will actively try to stop the Hero getting throughout the story.

You will have a stronger resolution at the end of your story if the audience can see that your hero has achieved his/her desire without any words being spoken.

2. Threat

The bad thing will happen to the character if they don't get this desire.

3. Action Steps To Achieve Desire:

In a very broad way, the actions the character will have to take to get this Goal, some large, some small. Each one completed being another step along the way to the goal. Each of these steps is extremely useful in generating story for your Beat Sheet.

4. Reward

The direct benefit of getting this Desire. It must matter enormously to the character.

5. Hero's Need

Now you need to work out what the Character *Needs*. This is something that is normally operating at the sub-conscious level in the character. They probably already have it when the story starts but they don't know it – and it only becomes apparent through the course of the story. This is often something that has been created by a deep trauma in the past of the character. Something terribly bad happened to them, a while back, and it scarred them, giving them a deep burning need for a certain sort of gratification.

The key is that this Need has to be in direct, powerful contradiction to their Desire. The things they want to do to satisfy this Need go in direct contradiction to the things they want to do to satisfy their Desire. This Need must run to the very end of the script. It's the invisible villain for our hero.

Maybe the hero is a man, and his mother was neglectful, or his first true love gave him the run around. This has left him with a Need to humiliate women. An obvious Desire to play against this would be that the Hero desperately wants a normal, loving relationship with a woman.

The job of this Hero Design Sheet is to split your main character in two. The job of the story is to put the hero into a position where this split becomes known and understood by the audience, and for them to be able to watch a widening and heightening of this split, until the final moments of the script, when the Hero makes his choice by taking the action[9] that indicates, once and for all, how they are going to settle; whether they are going to satisfy their Need, or their Desire.

---

[9] (and it should be an action – if it is done in a speech then you normally have a big problem with the story!!)

67

Most classic Superheroes have a Desire to hang up their fancy costume and mask and settle down with the person they love. They have a Need to be out in the world, living dangerously and beating the forces of evil. It's fairly easy to see where the conflict lies, and that's why the Villain pretty well always threatens the Hero's girl towards the end of the movie.

Having come up with this NEED then you should come up with:

6. Threat

7. Action Steps

8. Reward

for the Need, in the same way you did for the Desire.

Getting these rigorously worked out is dynamite. It leads to powerful and resonant stories. Very often taking a combination of the action steps for the Desire, and the action steps for the Need, will give you a lot of material for your story. Taking time to do this properly is great for generating your Battle Beats.

However, just as with the Logline, this design sheet is never set in stone. You must let it change through the course of designing your story.

For example, after you have done a draft of the beats for Act 2 you may come back here and find that the Needs and Desires you have sketched out no longer seem to apply. No problem. Just work out what the new ones are, and recreate your Sheet.

Top Tip: If you want to really create a powerful villain for your story then you should go through the same process for them. A villain that changes in the course of the story is a truly memorable villain – having Desire and Need for them makes it likely you will get this.

Minor Character Design Sheets

Sometimes when you are watching a movie, or an hour of TV, a character appears in one scene who has just a moment or two on screen but ends up being at least as memorable as the main characters. This is sometimes because of a brilliant performance by an actor, who takes a few bland words and invests them with all the weight of a vividly imagined and fascinating human life.

And sometimes, more relevant for us, it's down to the writing. But how do you write a memorable character when you only have a scene or two?

There is so much rubbish covering so many pages about how to generate characters. "Live their lives in your head". "Draw pictures of them". "Write 20 pages about their early childhood". "Write 20 pages about the way they look talk walk sing love drink eat smell..." On and on.

You don't need any of that. For a major character you need someone you have known and been fascinated by, plus several strong character oppositions; and for a minor character you need someone you have known and been fascinated by plus one strong character opposition.

OK. What do I mean by 'opposition'? It's like a contradiction, but not quite as strong. It's two opposing ways of being that come out in the same person often at almost the same time. If you know someone who everyone loves to talk about behind their backs, they will be full of oppositions.

Such as:

❖ A control freak who is constantly late for meetings.

❖ Someone with a massive ego, who secretly fears they are worthless.

❖ Someone with immense pride for a job that society thinks is ultimately low status.

❖ Someone who is warm, funny, and charismatic, yet is a helpless drug addict.

❖ An arrogant snob to his 'inferiors', who becomes a crawling, cringing coward when faced with those he believes are his betters.

❖ Someone who loves small fluffy animals, yet is capable of murdering children.

❖ Someone who is fiercely intelligent, yet can't crack the self assembly instructions for an Ikea cupboard.

❖ Someone who is fiercely intelligent but can't crack how to have meaningful relationships with other human beings.

❖ Someone who is aggressive, even confrontational about their sexuality, yet hasn't yet had the nerve to lose their virginity.

❖ Someone who is aggressive, even confrontational about their religious purity yet is having a wild affair with a married person behind everyone's backs.

On and on. The possibilities are literally endless. And each single opposition is gold for your characters.

The simple trick for creating memorable major characters (like your Hero) is to make sure you pick three or such oppositions for them. No more are necessary, and in fact might just confuse or blur the character.[10]

---

[10] I used to think the oppositions had to be in some way related – all perhaps to do with ego, or sexuality, or

70

And the trick for minor characters (the ones who only appear in one or a couple of scenes) is to make sure they have just one of these oppositions.

If you can write a scene where this minor character believably displays <u>both</u> halves of an opposition like this then you have created a character that the audience will like and remember.

In a nutshell: take the contradictions, feed them into the image and emotions you have in your head of the person you have known. Get this character to act and speak in accordance with the contradictions in their design, and there you have it – your memorable character pops up ready to wow your audience.

Cheat. Use Real People.

Oh, OK, OK. I confess. I do have one other tool I use when I'm really, really stuck. I look through magazines – not glossy celebrity laden stuff, but magazines dealing with real people. I look at all the people in there and look for people whose photo strikes me for some reason. The strength of their face. The terrible clothes. The look of blind hope. The fact they are innocent as hell but in a ton of trouble. Or sinful as they come. Whatever.

Sometimes just staring at a good character portrait will give you a mass of ideas for a character in your story.

The problem is that you can sometimes get such vivid ideas this way that you struggle to fit them in – but then that's a great problem to have.

---

whatever. In fact, some of the strongest characters I've created have been when I have just thrown together three apparently wildly unrelated contradictions into the same person and seen what happened.

71

If I really can't get the ideas in the current story, or they are threatening to pull the narrative somewhere you don't think it should go, then I just put them on ice and save them for another day.

Action Steps:

1.   For your Hero write down their Desire, and the Threat, Action Steps and Reward that go with that desire.

2.   Also for your Hero, write down their Need, and the Threat, Action Steps and Reward that go with that Need.

3.   For every significant Minor Character, write down a powerful character opposition.

4.   When you get stuck, look at random photos of real people for ideas.

Time taken: Ongoing.

Step 12: Assess Your Beat Sheet

So when you've done all that – and it can take weeks if you are doing it right – you will have a packed beat sheet. 60 or more lines, each line a single phrase, each line a story beat that makes you go, 'yep, that's GOOD!' when you think of it.

When you read this beat sheet you can see the story playing in your head. You're excited by it, you feel an adrenaline rush as you get to the end of the beat sheet. You know, in your heart of heart, it WORKS.

There is one last thing to do. Cut and paste all the beats in the sheet into a single column, in the order in which they will happen in your story.

This gives you your final story order

So now you can start writing your script, right?

Wrong.

Action Steps

1. Read your Beat Sheet.

2. Check you have all the Obligatory Beats in place.

3. Check that there is an unbroken flow through the sheet. No gaps. No bits you are ignoring, thinking, oh, I'll work that out when I come to write the script.

4. Make sure you like it. Does reading it excite you? Does it get your adrenaline flowing? It needs to.

Time taken. 10 minutes to 1 hour.

Step 13: Write Your Treatment

Oh, sure, you can go to script now if you insist, but 8 times out of 10 if you start writing scenes and dialogue at this point, before you know it you will be lost and bewildered in the middle of a sea of unconnected scenes, and then you'll start to flounder, and before you know it you've run out of steam and then you'll decide this system doesn't work and the whole thing stinks and you're going to join the army or maybe be an astronaut, either of which have to be less pain than writing a script.

The problem is that when you are writing scenes with dialogue you use a very different part of your brain to when you are building story.

Writing scenes is a very specific, focused activity, in which you take a particular story beat, and then you daydream, imagining yourself into that particular place with those particular people doing those particular things, to a point where you are actually inside their heads, hearing them speak, at a far finer grain than when you are just creating the story beat.

Coming out of that state of mind into what can be a very different following story beat and starting from scratch at that point can be very, VERY hard work.

It's much easier to come out from writing dialogue and find you have already done a large amount of the building work for the next beat.

So, to get this work done in the easiest way possible, now you have your Beat Sheet, before you write your script, you need to write your Treatment.

Copy your list of beats and put them into a word processor file. Make sure they are in the order they happen in.

Take the first beat in your list of beats. Go back to the pictures in your head that this beat conjures up, and write them down. Get the flavour of what's going on. Think about who is going to be in the beat, and the states of mind they might have. Think about what they want in the scene, and how they might try to get it. Think about the reactions of the other characters in the scene. Think about the sorts of things they might say. And take maybe ten minutes to do it.

It's as if you are writing a paraphrase of the scene without having to worry about coming up with snappy descriptions or dazzling dialogue.

That's all you have to do. You will come out with a short paragraph expanding that one sentence.

Now look at the next beat, and do the same.

Agony. I know. Keep going.

The beauty of this system is it actually by this stage if you have done the preparation properly this part may turn out to be an assembly job than real hard thinking. This is the place you can go and cut and paste all those notes you made when you were thinking about the script, all those fragments of dialogue, all those subtle explanations of what people were up to.

Continue till you have done the same for all the beats in your beat list.

This document is your Treatment.

Get Feedback? Not Always

Now, you have a choice:

❖ If you want you can get a gang of your friends to read the treatment. I'm certainly not a great fan of this – so often people just say random things, and badly judged comments about your script can throw you way off track. On the other hand, if three or more of them pick up on a point independently, you might just have a problem there. If enough people say something it could well be true, and it just might be worth thinking about ways to change the treatment to solve the problem.

❖ Or you might want to keep it entirely under your hat. Entirely up to you, and what you think of your friends' taste.

In movies you won't get any feedback at this point – people only want to see full drafts of screenplays. However in television the producer and the story editor/script editor will always want to go backwards and forwards on this treatment for what can seem like an interminable time, arguing over story points and generally battering the story into a shape that everyone feels works well.

Personally I'm very happy that this goes on, and indeed actively encourage the process. I want everybody who is powerful enough to be able to throw curve balls to actually throw them at this stage. It's so much easier to make story changes at this level compared to what it feels like after you have written a script and invested so much more love and time and care. [11]

---

[11] If you're writing a tv show bend over backwards, move heaven and hell, to get your Executive Producer to sign off on your treatment before you go to script. It makes it that much harder for them to sack you when you deliver the script if they've invested in your story at this stage.

Now, finally, (FINALLY!) you can start writing scenes and dialogue.

Action Steps

1. Copy and paste your Beat Sheet into your Word Processor.

2. Make sure each beat is in the right order.

3. For each beat, dream until you have the whole scene in your head. Write a prose paragraph (no dialogue) about what happens in that beat.

4. While you are doing that sling in all the relevant notes you have got on other scraps of paper, all the other thoughts that occur to you at this time.

For the record, if I write in single spaced, 12 point times Roman, with a double carriage return between paragraphs, I usually find each hour of screen time fills about 8-10 pages.

Time taken: 3 days – 1 week.

Step 14: Writing Scenes And Dialogue

This is where you start to use the third piece of software. Your screenwriting package.

Now, I suggest you go and buy this. They cost, for sure, but if you have genuinely got this far with your story, if you have really put this solid amount of work into the whole thing, then you are clearly committed to being a writer, and you may as well use proper writer's tools. If you are really broke, you could soldier on with your word processor, but having one of these two packages will make your life so much easier.

The market leaders are, in my mind, Movie Magic Screenwriter, and Final Draft. They are both terrific - and I do find them both to have the occasional glitch. No show stoppers in either case, but they both sometimes do funny things when you least expect it. Just pick the one that looks good to you.

Dream Before You Write

Pick the first paragraph in your treatment. Think about it over and over again, visualise it in the bath, when you wake up, when you are walking along the street. Visualise what happens until you can run it through like a little movie in your mind, seeing what happens, almost hearing the dialogue. This will be your first sequence.

Write

Get that sequence down now. Write the scenes. Make the characters move, and talk, and feel.

Repeat

Dream, and Write, over and over again, until you have reached the end of your treatment.

You have just finished your first draft.

Congratulate Yourself

Format it. Print it. Weigh it in your hand. Admire it. You should be proud. Few people get this far. And if you followed these steps, it's going to be far more readable than anything else you have written.

So that's it. Draft 1. Done and written.

Oh. You expected more?

Well, I'm not going to waste your time by telling you how to lay out your scenes on the page so they look like a film script – you can find that stuff anywhere on the internet.

More to the point, I'm also not going to give you any more detailed advice as to how to write these scenes, because there isn't any to give.

It's down to you, and whether you take the time to create vivid dreams of these scenes and sequences. If you have them in your head they will transcribe without any fuss.

I do, however, have some Rules of Thumb.

Rules of Thumb

❖ Make sure your dialogue never, ever says what the person is actually thinking. That's called being On The Nose, and there are few worse sins. The dialogue should almost play the opposite of what's going on. It

80

should be oblique, apparently ignoring the real stakes of the scene; and be about anything other than what the person is actually thinking deep down.

Bad drama is FULL of people standing around telling each other what they are really thinking. Good drama uses subtext constantly.

❖ "Get into the scene as late as you can, make your point, and get out as early as you can."

Old advice, as vital as ever. Don't worry that being so brief seems unrealistic. Look at any drama on TV. People aren't realistic in drama. Being realistic in this sense is boring. That really does mean don't bother with 'Hello', How are you' and 'Goodbye' - unless you are consciously using them to tell us something interesting about the character. It also means looking hard at the start and end of your scenes to see what could go. (It can go if the story – i.e. the emotional skeleton of the script - stays the same without it.)

❖ You can break that rule if your dialogue is funny. You can usually take time out from strict story telling if you are being funny. But don't be too long about it unless you are writing a real full blooded comedy.

❖ Be concise. Short and to the point. Don't give us endless flowery description. You aren't painting a detailed picture of every aspect of this world, that's the director's job. You are providing the emotional lines of the script, the skeleton.

So: 'The space ship hangs in space' rather than 'The alien craft seems suspended in star strewn blackness.'

❖ The same goes for dialogue. It's an old BBC rule that you need an extremely good reason for a speech to last more than four lines in standard screenplay format. Characters in American drama tend to be more articulate than characters in British drama, but

81

it's a great target to aim for whichever side of the Atlantic you are.

❖ Track each character who speaks in the scene. Find out who is driving the scene, (normally the one who <u>really</u> wants something), and make sure that they end the scene in a different emotional state to when they came in.

❖ Never put directions for the Camera. If you want us to look at something, just give us a phrase or two that tells us about it. We'll get the idea.

❖ Don't give the actors their blocking. That is, don't write down every time they smile, sit, stand, or otherwise move their body. Again, it's something actors like to discover themselves, and it gets in the way when you are reading the script.

❖ If you want to stay cool, don't ever tell the actors how to deliver their lines. That is, never use those little instructions in brackets after a character's name to tell the actor and the director how to say the line. Believe me, 99% of the time they are completely unnecessary.

I once wandered into a room where a director and an actor were laughing themselves stupid over a script. (Not mine.) They were going through the script, reading the parts aloud, and acting out the redundant parentheticals with massively over zealous conviction. So it was something like:

```
        Robert:
      (passionately)
     Rose, I love you!


         Rose
    (shy and reluctant)
  But I only met you half an
  hour ago. I don't know you.


        Robert
       (raging)
  Since when did what you
  think mattered?
```

Imagine that, read without mercy, by two pros hamming it up to the max. Painful? Very. Funny? Extremely. Would the writer have minded? Totally. Just don't give these evil minded people the chance…

OK, so it wasn't very kind of them, but it was a very valid point. Actors and Directors work out how to read the lines you have written, that's their job. If you're lucky they will do it in a wonderfully subtle way that will surprise and delight you.

Action Steps

For each paragraph in your treatment:

1. Sink into a waking dream about it. Run it through in your head until it becomes real to you.

2. Write down what you see and hear in your Screenwriting Software.

3. Obey the Rules of Thumb.

Time taken: Approx two weeks for every hour of screen time. (Any less, and you will probably find that at any given point you are reaching for the first cliché that pops into your head, instead of mining the deep psychological truths and images of the situation.)

Summary

And there we have it. Fourteen steps that, if you follow them diligently, can change your writing process, can give a kick start to your writing to the point where people are hungry to read your scripts.

Which IS what you want, isn't it?

I'm really excited about this book. It took a long time to write. I'm utterly serious when I say that the long lead time was a result of me not wanting to short change anyone. Before I would publish I had to do a real analysis job on myself to find out what I actually did while I was writing.

As a result, Screenwriting Goldmine is the only screenwriting book I've ever seen that goes into so much nitty gritty, so much focused insider detail.

It's the real thing. It works for me. I'm sure it will work for you.

Come and tell me what you think. Email me at

info@screenwritinggoldmine.com

Also, when you get stuck do wander over to the website at www.screenwritinggoldmine.com

There's a mass of additional free information up there, including in depth audio interviews with industry professionals, more How To Articles, plus a very active forum full of like minded screenwriters, who are always very happy to critique each other's scripts. Plus, as I never tire of saying, networking is everything in this game, and you never know who you might meet in there...

APPENDIX 1

12 CRITICAL QUESTIONS TO STRAIGHTEN OUT YOUR STORY

THE SCREENWRITING GOLDMINE CRIBSHEET FOR PEOPLE IN A HURRY

INTRODUCTION

I firmly believe the method I've just detailed is a Class A, supercharged method to produce the best, most commercial, most reader-energising version of your story possible.

But I'm also a realist. I recognise that my way takes a lot of work, and sometimes you just want a quick fix.

If you're feeling lazy, I've put together twelve questions to get you into the right ballpark with your story.

If doing all the steps of my method seems like climbing Everest in flip flops right now, then the very least I can do is push you out for a quick jog round the screenwriting park.

In NO WAY are these questions any kind of substitute for the extended process.

But I guess they're slightly better than nothing, and if you answer them fully then you'll be in a better place to do the whole method when you feel more energetic.

Don't start writing till you have written down answers to all twelve! I mean it!

THE 12 QUESTIONS

1. Whose story is it?

(Clue, it <u>should</u> be the character you are most interested in, and it is <u>definitely</u> the one who makes the choice in step 10.)

2. What emotional state are they in when your story starts?

(Describe this in a single phrase. No extended paragraphs. 'Farmhand.' 'Down and out'. 'Unmotivated teenager')

3. What do they want?

(This is what they will be chasing through the entire script, and the script will end when they finally get it, or finally don't get it. It should be something concrete, in the material world. Avoid vague ideas like Happiness, or Love. The real test you should apply is asking yourself whether, when they get it, we can see them getting it in a picture.)

4. What is the inciting incident, and why does it affect them more than anyone else?

(What sets the story running? What is the event that makes them want what they want? Why does this event affect them so deeply?)

5. Who is trying to stop them getting what they want?

(Clue, this is your Villain, and they should be behind most of the problems the Hero encounters.)

6. What obstacles does your Villain put in Hero's path?

7. What will your Hero lose if they don't achieve their objective?

8. What are the two big story twists that end Acts 1 and 2?

(The second and third tent poles in the Screenwriting Goldmine method. The best way to think about these twists is to see them as points where the hero learns surprising new information, that puts them in a new emotional state, and which increases the urgency with they will pursue their desire from question 3.)

9. What do they learn that they were wrong about at the start of the story?

(Crucial for powerful story telling. It means the Hero can grow emotionally over the course of the story.)

10. What is the massive choice that the character has to make at the end of the script that decides which way the story ends?

(Clue, you must be able to demonstrate this choice visually.)

11. What emotional state is the character in at the end of the story?

(Again, one word, or a single short phrase. 'Hero'. 'Magnate'. 'Crime Boss'. It must be a million miles away from their state at the beginning of the story. The journey between these two states is the character's 'Arc'.)

12. Why should we care about any of this?

(Make sure there is at least one dominant character for whom we feel extreme affection – and make very bad things happen to them.)

NOTES

Made in the USA
Lexington, KY
23 February 2010